W9-BVI-979

museum **highlights**

CONTENTS

The Rhinebeck Panorama (detail), c.1806
This spectacular view invites us to imagine that we are viewing London from a balloon above the Thames. The anonymous watercolour was discovered lining a barrel of pistols in Rhinebeck, New York, in 1941.

FOREWORD

Welcome to the Museum of London.

I am delighted that you have chosen to visit us and hope that you will find much to enjoy and reflect on whilst you are here. The subject of this Museum is London, one of the world's greatest cities and a place that touches everyone in some form, whether you live in London or are just visiting. This is your story just as much as ours.

These are exciting times for the Museum of London. The institution is over 30 years old (our building opened in 1976) and the twenty-first century has already seen many changes. In 2002 we opened a second site, the Museum of London Docklands. In 2009 we opened the Clore Learning Centre, a new suite of education rooms to serve the many schools that use our resources. In 2010 we refurbished the entire lower floor of the building to create the new Galleries of Modern London, and a new setting for the Lord Mayor's Coach.

All these changes are designed to keep our stories fresh, our visitor-experience excellent and our creativity buzzing. The Museum of London must reflect the values of London itself, a city of diversity and energy where creativity thrives.

Enjoy your visit.

Professor Jack Lohman
Director, Museum of London

Woodcut from the Chronicle of England, 1497

NVM·AVGG
DEOMARTICA
MVLO·TIBERINI
VSCELERIANVS
C·BELL·
MORITIX·
LONDINIENSI
VM·
MVS

Fragment of a Roman building inscription
This is the earliest known mention of London recorded on a Roman inscription.

A MUSEUM FOR LONDONERS

The Museum of London was opened by Her Majesty Queen Elizabeth II on 2 December 1976. The first new museum building to open in London since the Second World War, it attracted 370,000 visitors in its first six months and instantly acquired a reputation for excellence: 'no other museum in Britain received such all round glowing reports from our visitors', said *The Good Museums Guide*.

The new institution brought together two older museums: the London Museum and the Guildhall Museum. Both had lost their premises during the war, so uniting them was an inspired step. From its beginning, the new Museum saw itself as 'not simply of or about London, but also for London' Its mission then and now is to play a part in the lives of all Londoners, 'to inspire a passion for London'.

The collections and the permanent galleries tell the story of London's development as a city over hundreds of thousands of years: from prehistoric settlements in the Thames Valley, through the founding of 'Londinium' by the Roman army, to the great world city that London is today. How did London come to be such an extraordinary place? Who were the Londoners who lived here in the past? What does the future hold? The Museum explores all these questions and more. It is a truly remarkable story.

Union (Horse with two Discs), 2001
This intriguing sculpture by Christopher Le Brun stands at the Museum's entrance. The two discs are said to stand for night and day, and the horse symbolises journeys.

THE MUSEUM'S COLLECTIONS

In 1976 the newly opened Museum boasted of its 'half a million objects'. Since then numbers have grown, and many nationally important items have entered the collections.

Today, the Museum has around one million items in its core collection, plus an additional six million 'finds', some in fragments dug up as part of archaeological excavations. All human life is represented in these objects, from a Roman 'bikini' worn by a female athlete, to a suitcase carried by a Turkish Cypriot man when he arrived in London as a refugee. The collections are constantly growing as archaeological digs unearth new discoveries; and the Museum gathers objects from today's London, as a record of life in the twenty-first-century city.

ABOVE: *From Pentonville Road looking West: Evening, 1884*
This painting by John O'Connor shows the distinctive bulk of the Midland Railway Hotel, opened in 1873 at St Pancras Station.

OPPOSITE TOP:
A tin toy
One of the thousand penny toys given to the London Museum by Ernest King in 1918. King bought his toys from the street peddlers who traditionally sold them on Ludgate Hill just before Christmas.

OPPOSITE BOTTOM:
Roman Glass Bowl
Found in a Roman cemetery at Aldgate, this rare example of mosaic glass shows how one Roman Londoner was accompanied on their journey to the underworld.

The Museum holds:

- 25,000 items of clothing and fashion
- 100,000 paintings, prints and photographs of London
- Europe's largest archaeological archive including 17,000 excavated skeletons
- 50,000 objects from the prehistoric period and Roman London
- 15,000 objects from Saxon and medieval London
- 55,000 objects from Tudor and Stuart London

- 110,000 objects from modern London (the 18th to the 20th centuries)
- 1,800 life stories from individual Londoners
- Half a million historic documents, including the archives of the Port of London Authority
- A growing collection of items from the 21st century, including websites, film and items related to the 2012 Olympic Games

To find out more about the Museum's collections visit www.museumoflondon.org.uk

LONDON BEFORE LONDON

The Museum's oldest objects date back to a time when London was nothing but tundra, and the local population would fit on a double-decker bus. They shed light on the thousands of years before London became a city, from around 450,000 BC to the arrival of the Roman legions in AD 50.

During these centuries the Thames valley was occupied by several different human species, all sharing the landscape with a range of animals. The earliest of these peoples lived as nomadic hunter-gatherers but as ways of life changed, so recognisable settlements emerged. These early people left behind an array of fascinating things – human and animal bones, stone tools and, later in the period, finely worked metal vessels and weapons.

The river Thames was central to the lives of the people who lived along its banks. The Museum's collections include over 300 objects dredged from the river's depths – many of them bronze and iron swords, laid there to please the gods of the water.

Lower jaw and tooth of a mammoth
Herds of mammoth would have been a common sight in the Thames valley from around 200,000 years ago. The lower jaw is from Ilford and the tooth from Whitehall.

Alderwood club, 3600–3300 BC
Found on the Thames foreshore at Chelsea this two-handed club would have delivered a fearful blow. Many skulls found in tombs of the period show signs of head injuries.

The flintknapper's craft, 300,000–2000 BC
Thousands of skilfully made flint tools and weapons have been found across London. Freshly knapped flint was both aesthetically pleasing and extremely sharp.

**Flint adze,
8000–4000 BC**
An unusually large adze
made of handsomely
banded flint. Probably
too large to have been
mounted effectively on a
wooden haft, this may
have been intended for
the gods.

**Handmade pottery bowl,
3000 BC**
Found during excavations
at Heathrow Airport in
1944. Carefully decorated
bowls such as these would
have been used for
cooking and storage.

**Face of a woman,
3600–3100 BC**
Reconstructed from the
skull found in a burial at
Shepperton, scientific
analysis of the bone showed
that the woman had died in
her thirties and probably far
from her birthplace.

**Daggers from the Thames,
2000–1500 BC**
Many daggers of flint, bronze
and iron have been found in
the river. The representation
of a dagger made of bone (left)
is particularly unusual.

**Iron dagger and sheath,
6th century BC**
While this dagger blade
from the Thames at
Mortlake was probably
imported from central
Europe, its banded
bronze sheath is the work
of a British armourer.

**Cast bronze swords,
1100–800 BC**
A small selection of the
many leaf-shaped swords
dredged from the west
London Thames. Some may
have been lost in local
skirmishes; others were
probably gifted to the river.

**Bronze looped palstave
axe, 1400–1200 BC**
Cast bronze axe from the
Thames at Richmond. Such
axes were probably used to
clear local woodland for the
laying out of riverside fields
and settlements.

**Bronze pegged spearhead,
1420–1100 BC**
Large spearhead from the
Thames at Hammersmith.
Remains of its apple wood
shaft survived in the socket,
allowing it to be
scientifically dated.

Bronze coins of Cunobelin, AD 10–40
Cunobelin (Shakespeare's Cymbaline) was a British tribal leader who ruled parts of southern Britain in the first century AD. His death provided the Romans with a pretext for invasion in AD 43.

Blue glass bead, 2nd–1st century BC
This blue glass bead with yellow and white trailed decoration from the Thames at Richmond probably formed part of a prized necklace.

Bronze-bound wooden tankard, 1st century BC/AD
This splendid tankard from the Thames at Kew has a capacity of over two litres (four pints). Such vessels were probably passed round at communal feasts.

ROMAN LONDON

The Roman occupation of Britain heralded the foundation of London as a settlement, following the annexation of Britain as a province of the Roman Empire in AD 43. With the new settlement growing on both sides of the Thames (in what is now the City and Southwark), Londinium became the communication and administrative hub and a trading emporium that served the burgeoning province.

The first Londinium was totally destroyed in AD 60, during the uprising of the tribes led by Queen Boudica, but was quickly rebuilt so that by AD 100 it had become the largest and most influential city in the province. At its height, it boasted a thriving port, a large forum and basilica, public baths and a fort which housed soldiers working for the military administration. The amphitheatre, religious complexes and temples served the spiritual needs of Roman Londoners, a cultural mix of diverse nationalities from around the empire.

The Museum's Roman collections, among the finest in the country, have been much enriched in recent years as the spate of new office building in London has enabled archaeologists to unearth both unique treasures as well as evidence of everyday life.

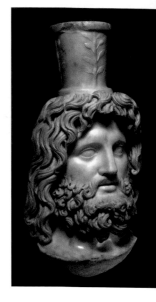

Head of Serapis
Marble head of the Romano-Egyptian god of the Underworld. Wearing a corn measure on his head to symbolise agricultural fertility, he came from a group of sculptures from the Temple of Mithras.

Novelty oil lamp
Small ceramic lamp depicting a human foot wearing a sandal. The lamp, an early import into Roman London, once had a wick burning in the hole in the big toe.

Ribbed bowl

Cast blue glass bowl. Minerals, such as cobalt, produced the prized deep blue during the glass-making process and such vessels were expensive imports for the luxury market.

Perfume bottle

Barrel-shaped container for perfumed oils. Made by Frontinus Sextinus in the Rhineland provinces of the Roman Empire, the vessel would have been a fancy container for a highly prized import.

Mercury with ram and tortoise

The marble messenger of the gods sits on a rock, holding a money-bag. The ram symbolises fertility and the tortoise, through music from tortoise-shell lyres, the eternal happiness of the afterlife.

Bacchic group
Marble scene showing a group of revellers supporting the central figure, a drunken Bacchus. As god of wine, the inscription below praises Bacchus for 'giving life to wandering mortals'.

Venus figurine
Pipeclay image of the goddess of love and fertility. Made in France, this would have been bought as payment to the gods for fulfilling a vow to be lucky in love.

Figure of Hercules
Known for his Herculean labours, which included the slaying of a lion, this bronze Hercules is shown wearing the lion skin as the symbol of his success.

Hairpin
Long bone pin, terminating in a female bust with an ornate coiffure. Such pins were needed to hold the hairstyles of the day in place. Similar pins are shown around the top of the head.

Comb and manicure set
Ornate bone comb and bronze manicure set used for personal hygiene. The manicure set consists of implements for keeping nails manicured, for removing excess hair and for mixing and applying make-up.

Military belt fittings
Bronze belt set, finely decorated with spiral motifs and animal heads. Its style indicates a wearer who was probably a high-ranking German military official working for the late-Roman administration.

Necklaces
One of these necklaces, made from amber beads from the Baltic, is still strung on its original thread while the other, made of gold wire links, includes emeralds from Roman Egypt.

Examples of 'face' pots
Ceramic vessels with human faces. Such vessels, found in cemeteries and religious areas, are thought to have been votive offerings but it is unknown what the faces were meant to portray.

Canister and strainer
Silver-gilt cylindrical container decorated with figures of men and animals. It has an internal silver perforated strainer, probably used for infusing herbs or drugs as part of the Mithraic rituals.

Engraved depiction of Pegasus
Banded agate intaglio, for use as a seal in a signet ring, depicting the mythical winged horse. It was found in a jeweller's shop, destroyed in the Boudican rebellion of AD 60.

Coin of the Emperor Hadrian
Gold aureus, one of a hoard found hidden under the floor of a substantial building in Fenchurch Street. Such coins, never in everyday circulation, would have been used for large business transactions.

Word die
Basalt die with pigment-filled letters that correspond to the numbers on normal dice. The type of word-game is unknown but 'Italia' (Italy) was equal to a throw of six.

MEDIEVAL LONDON

The Museum's medieval collections illuminate a long period of history, from the Anglo-Saxon settlement in the fifth century, through Viking raids and the Norman Conquest of 1066, to the splendour and bustle of London under Tudor rule, and the dramatic consequences of Henry VIII's dissolution of the monasteries.

This was the period when London's merchants and craftsmen consolidated their position as privileged citizens, banding together in crafts, guilds and parishes to create a system of self-government that still survives today, particularly through the office of the Lord Mayor of London, which dates back to 1189.

London grew rich as a trading centre, its population reaching a peak of perhaps as much as 100,000 by 1300, only to be decimated by the Black Death (bubonic plague) which raged through Europe in the 1340s. The city's appearance also changed. Saxon houses were simple and built from wood, wattle and daub. Typical medieval houses were tall and narrow, with the upper storeys overhanging into the street. The main landmarks in medieval London were churches, their towers and spires creating a distinctive skyline. Tallest of all was St Paul's Cathedral, a colossal building and the largest in medieval Britain.

Gilded silver brooch, early 500s
Although made in southern England this brooch shows strong Scandinavian influences. It was found in the grave of a young Saxon woman to the south of London.

Silver penny, c.880
This penny was minted in London around 880. One side shows the head of Alfred the Great and the other a monogram of 'LVNDONIA' – the medieval Latin for 'London'.

Copper-alloy, gold and garnet brooch, mid 600s
Found in a grave during excavations in Floral Street, Covent Garden, this brooch would have belonged to an aristocratic Anglo-Saxon lady. Floral Street lies in the heart of the early Saxon settlement of Lundenwic.

Viking weapons, early 1000s
In the late 900s and early 1000s London was under attack by the Vikings. At one point they pulled down London Bridge. These Viking weapons were found near the Bridge.

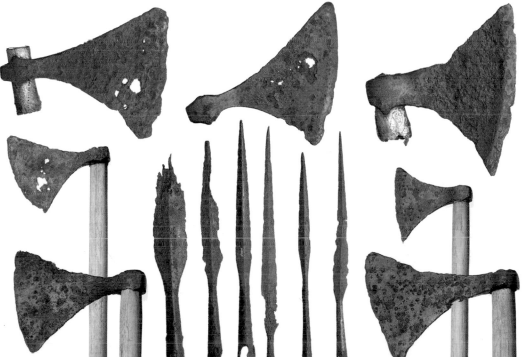

Face pot, early 1300s
Is this the face of a medieval potter? It appears on a jug made in Kingston to the south of London. Face pots were very popular at this time.

Medieval pottery
Large quantities of pottery vessels were imported into London. They were made in the area around London but also in France and northern Europe.

Glass beaker, about 1300
Intended for wine, this fine Venetian beaker is decorated with coloured enamel. The shield with a blue wolf shows the arms of the Wolfsberg family who held land near Augsburg in southern Germany.

Bone mount, mid 1300s
This mount may have decorated a wooden panel. The young knight is kneeling with his sword at his side.

Stone corbel, 1300s
A corbel from the Temple Church, off Fleet Street. It depicts a fashionable young woman wearing a wimple or neck cloth under her chin.

Hanging lamp, 1100s
The shape of this lamp is similar to the traditional shape of a Jewish 'Sabbath lamp'. London had a thriving Jewish community until it was expelled in 1290.

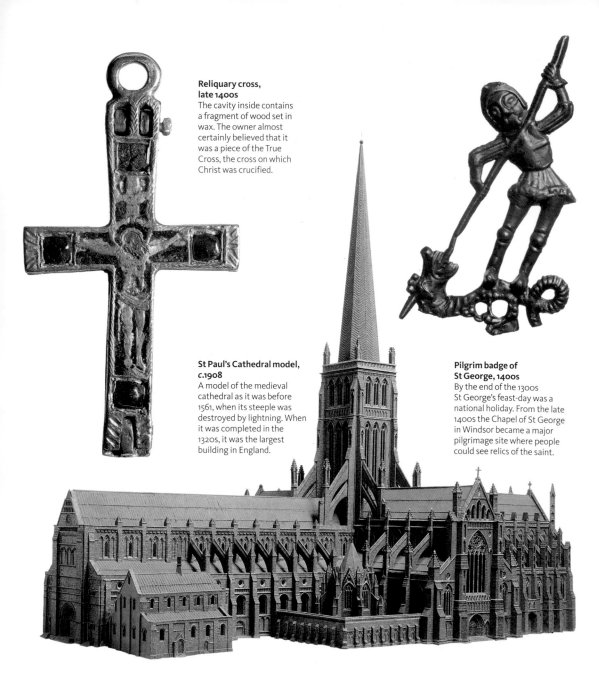

**Reliquary cross,
late 1400s**
The cavity inside contains
a fragment of wood set in
wax. The owner almost
certainly believed that it
was a piece of the True
Cross, the cross on which
Christ was crucified.

**St Paul's Cathedral model,
c.1908**
A model of the medieval
cathedral as it was before
1561, when its steeple was
destroyed by lightning. When
it was completed in the
1320s, it was the largest
building in England.

**Pilgrim badge of
St George, 1400s**
By the end of the 1300s
St George's feast-day was a
national holiday. From the
late 1400s the Chapel of St George
in Windsor became a major
pilgrimage site where people
could see relics of the saint.

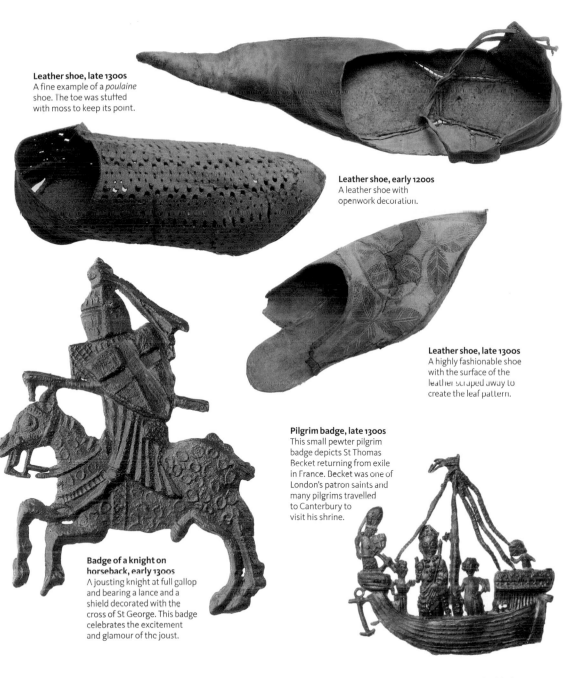

Leather shoe, late 1300s
A fine example of a *poulaine* shoe. The toe was stuffed with moss to keep its point.

Leather shoe, early 1200s
A leather shoe with openwork decoration.

Leather shoe, late 1300s
A highly fashionable shoe with the surface of the leather scraped away to create the leaf pattern.

Pilgrim badge, late 1300s
This small pewter pilgrim badge depicts St Thomas Becket returning from exile in France. Becket was one of London's patron saints and many pilgrims travelled to Canterbury to visit his shrine.

Badge of a knight on horseback, early 1300s
A jousting knight at full gallop and bearing a lance and a shield decorated with the cross of St George. This badge celebrates the excitement and glamour of the joust.

Maiolica vase from Tuscany, *c.*1510
Vases with the 'YHS' trigram (from the Greek word for Jesus) were imported into London for devotional use. Several have been excavated from the sites of pre-Reformation religious houses.

Jerkin, *c.*1550–1600
These practical, decorative garments were highly fashionable from the mid-1500s. Those made from Spanish leather were particularly prized.

German stoneware, 1550s
Decorative relief-moulded stonewares from Cologne begin to appear in London by *c.*1510. These were expensive consumer products and were designed to appeal to the luxury end of the market.

Paternoster bead, early 1500s

This bead symbolises the transience of life. Carved with a woman's head on one side and a 'death's head' on the other, it was used as an aid to prayer.

Annunciation altarpiece, c.1500

The 'wings' of a triptych altarpiece depicting the Angel Gabriel with the arms of Westminster Abbey (left), and the Virgin Mary with the arms of Abbot George Fascet (right).

WAR, PLAGUE AND FIRE 1550s–1660s

By the 1550s London was a wealthy city, but an uneasy one. The last Tudor monarch, Queen Elizabeth I, held power but religion still divided loyalties, and England remained vulnerable to invasion or insurrection.

This was the London that William Shakespeare knew. The Museum's collections include items related to the Rose Theatre, which stood on the south side of the river at Bankside from 1587 to 1605. Many of the greatest playwrights of the day had works performed at the Rose, and William Shakespeare acted on its stage.

By the 1640s ideological tensions had split England into warring factions. London became the stage for some of the Civil War's most traumatic events, in particular the execution of King Charles I, who was tried for treason and beheaded in public on Tuesday 30 January 1649. The watching crowd is said to have let out a low moan.

London from Southwark, c.1630 (detail)
This is the earliest known painted view of London. It shows Old London Bridge, the Tower of London and the spires of the City churches.

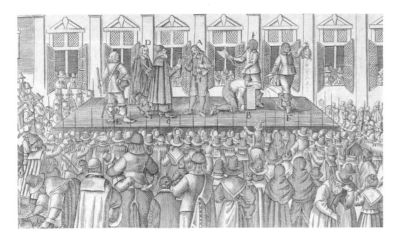

The execution of Charles I, 1649
Londoners flocked to witness the execution of Charles I on 30 January 1649. The king was executed on a makeshift scaffold outside the Banqueting House in Whitehall.

Charles I with his head stitched back on, c.1660
This painting represents Charles as a saintly martyr. The three lamenting women with their crowns falling symbolise England, Scotland and Ireland.

Commemorative plate, dated 1600
This is the earliest dated commemorative piece of English delftware, and the first known with an English inscription. It was made in Aldgate by Flemish refugee potters.

Copperplate maps, c.1558
This engraved map of London is the earliest known view of the City. The plates (detail right, and below) cover an area from Shoreditch to London Bridge.

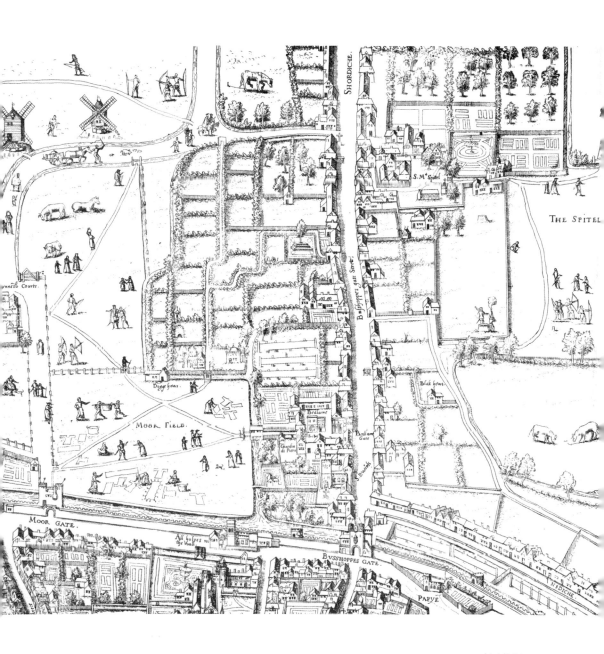

SHORDICE.

S. M. Spitel

THE SPITEL

Bysshoppes gate Strete

Woodnesb Courte

Dogg hows

Blak hows

MOOR FIELD.

Bedlame

Bedlam Gate

Giardino di Pietri

MOOR GATE.

All hallowes in the Wall

BYSSHOPPES GATE.

PAPYE

N DICHE

Oliver Cromwell's death mask, 1658
This plaster cast was made from a wax impression of Cromwell's head. His funeral was lavish, and wood and wax effigies of him were placed in Somerset House for the lying-in-state.

Coronation mug, 1660
This souvenir mug was made to celebrate the Restoration of Charles II to the throne in 1660. It was used for caudle, a hot spicy drink of ale or wine.

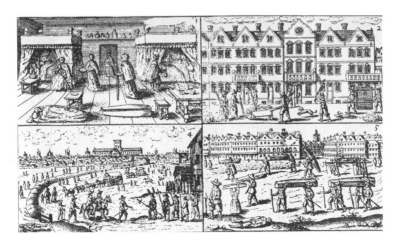

More troubles were yet to come. In 1665 plague raged through the city, killing up to 7,000 a week. The following year London suffered its most famous disaster: the Great Fire of 1666. Beginning on 2 September, the fire raged for four days, destroying four-fifths of the buildings within the old City walls. It was a cataclysmic event which still resonates in Londoners' minds today.

The Great Plague of 1665
This bell was rung to announce the collection of the dead. The illustration, from a Mortality Bill, shows Londoners fleeing the city, and victims in their homes.

The Great Fire of London, 1666
The Great Fire was the most destructive fire England has ever seen. After five days, 13,200 homes had gone and four-fifths of the City was destroyed

Fireman's helmet, late 1600s
The City churches kept fire-fighting equipment for emergency use. This helmet, painted 'BB' and 'GB', was probably used by the parish of St Botolph and St George Billingsgate.

Ring and Brooch, early 1600s
These jewels form part of the Cheapside Hoard, a cache of 400 gems and other precious objects discovered by workmen in 1912.

EXPANDING CITY 1660s–1850s

The years following the Great Fire heralded the start of a new chapter in London's story. The city expanded on the ground and its influence spread across the globe. London became capital not only of a 'united kingdom' but also of a vast empire. In size and population, wealth and power, there had never been a city like it.

All aspects of London grew phenomenally from 1666. Printing presses multiplied and Londoners developed an appetite for newspapers, ideas and debate. London was also Britain's largest manufacturing centre, noted particularly for its specialist products such as watches and scientific instruments. By the 1850s Queen Victoria was on the throne and London housed a Great Exhibition, promoting England as the 'workshop of the world'. By now London had long overtaken Paris as Europe's largest city. It was a busy and chaotic place, a confident city that thrived on free enterprise. People were drawn to London from all parts of the world and the massive new docks handled unprecedented quantities of cargo.

This London was a city of amusement as well as hardship. Pleasure gardens, theatres and music halls thrived in the capital, alongside workshops, warehouses and prisons.

Nelson's sword of honour, 1798
The Corporation of London presented this honorary sword and the Freedom of the City to Admiral Lord Nelson in 1800 to mark his victory at the Battle of the Nile.

Panorama of London, detail of Old London Bridge, 1749 Samuel and Nathaniel Buck
This engraving, one of five, forms part of a long panorama of the north bank of the Thames from Westminster to the Tower of London.

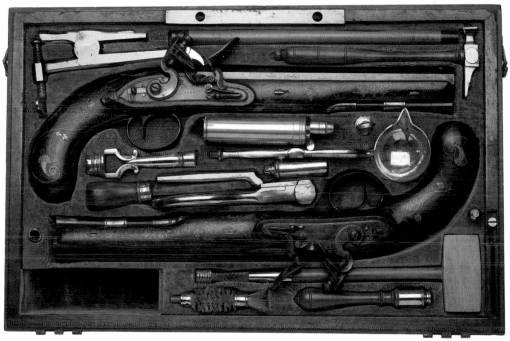

Duelling Pistols by Toms, *c.*1810
These flintlock duelling pistols belonged to a captain in the Hackney Volunteer Riflemen, a militia established in London during the Napoleonic Wars.

Commemorative gold ring with miniature medals of Prince Albert and Queen Victoria, 1840
Six dozen of these rings were made for Queen Victoria's marriage.

Gold and enamel cased watch made by Jefferys and Jones, *c.*1781
Many costly and intricate London-made watches were exported to Europe, Turkey and the colonies.

The Cockpit, **William Hogarth, 1759**

Cockfighting was London's most popular sport at this time. The venue in Hogarth's engraving is the Royal Cockpit near St James's Park. The central figure is the blind aristocrat, Lord Albemarle Bertie.

The Idle 'Prentice Executed at Tyburn, **William Hogarth, 1747**

Taken from the 'Industry and Idleness' series, this engraving shows the hanging of Tom Idle for highway robbery. London's public executions drew enormous crowds and shops would close for the occasion.

Southwark Fair, **William Hogarth, 1733**

Hogarth's engraving depicts a typical London street fair. Entertainers of various kinds can be seen, including actors, acrobats, street musicians and a magician. Gambling and petty crime are also evident.

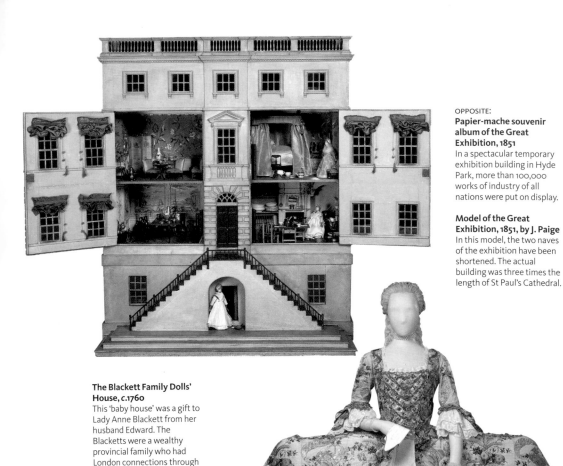

OPPOSITE:
Papier-mache souvenir album of the Great Exhibition, 1851
In a spectacular temporary exhibition building in Hyde Park, more than 100,000 works of industry of all nations were put on display.

Model of the Great Exhibition, 1851, by J. Paige
In this model, the two naves of the exhibition have been shortened. The actual building was three times the length of St Paul's Cathedral.

The Blackett Family Dolls' House, c.1760
This 'baby house' was a gift to Lady Anne Blackett from her husband Edward. The Blacketts were a wealthy provincial family who had London connections through Edward's involvement in commerce and politics.

Anne Fanshawe's dress, c.1751
This spectacular dress is made from brocaded silk, woven in Spitalfields. The dress was made for Anne Fanshawe, the daughter of Crisp Gascoyne, a merchant who became Lord Mayor of London in 1752.

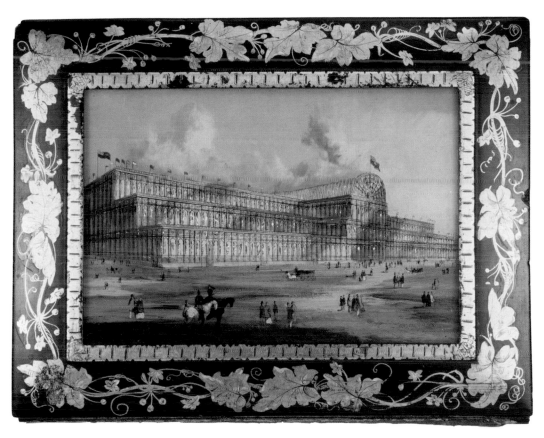

OPPOSITE:
Eastward Ho!, August 1857,
Henry Nelson O'Neil
Soldiers are shown boarding
a ship at Gravesend, leaving
to fight in the 'Indian Mutiny',
the first Indian war of
independence.

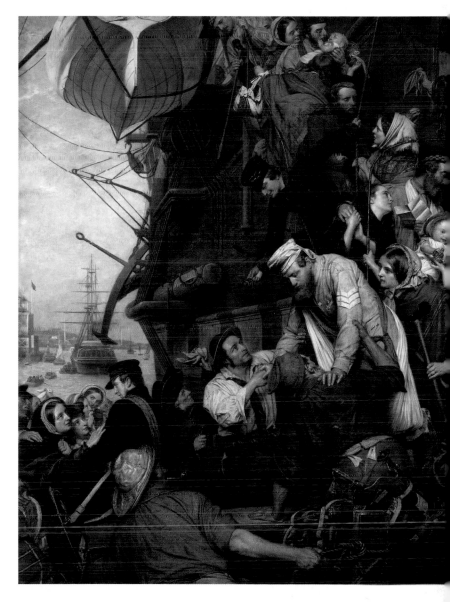

Home Again, 1858,
Henry Nelson O'Neil
Here, in the companion work
to *Eastward Ho!*, it is one year
later and the same soldiers
are returning home, being
greeted by family and friends.

THE VICTORIAN WALK

The look and feel of London around 1900 is vividly evoked in one part of the Museum's galleries. The shop fronts, fixtures and fittings in 'the Victorian Walk' are all original and come from buildings demolished in the 1960s or 1970s.

   The shops include a pub, a tobacconist's, a barber's, a chemist, a grocer's, a tailor's and a pawnbroker's. There is also a bank office and a recreation of the showroom of the London glass manufacturers, James Powell & Sons, who produced their famous 'Whitefriars' glass from a working glasshouse in the City of London until the 1920s. The glass inside the showroom was all made by Whitefriars.

OPPOSITE:
The Barber
The barber's shop has original fittings from several shops, including Pottle's in Upper Street, Islington. The copper towel heater dispensed steaming towels to soothe the skin after a close shave.

The Tobacconist
The shop fittings in this reconstruction are from Redford's tobacconist shop in Clerkenwell. The wooden Highlander and Blackamoor figures advertised the sale of Scottish snuff and American tobacco.

PEOPLE'S CITY 1850s–1950s

By the 1850s London was the world's wealthiest city. But success had come at the expense of its people. Overcrowding and sanitation problems divided the city, whose rich and poor lived in separate worlds.

As the social divide widened, so concerns deepened and the need for action became more urgent. A new system of local government began to tackle the city's massive problems of poverty, housing and health. The Suffragette demand for 'Votes for women!' was one of many campaigns that brought political debate on to London's streets.

Technology quickened change as Londoners became accustomed to electricity, telephones, motor vehicles and moving pictures. A housing boom created new suburbs, enabling London to spread its boundaries and form the outline shape of Greater London as we know it today.

By 1939, one in five of the British population lived in the

OPPOSITE:
The Arrest of Emmeline Pankhurst, 1914
This photograph shows the Suffragette leader Emmeline Pankhurst being arrested outside Buckingham Palace as she attempts to present a petition to the King in support of female suffrage.

Behind the Bar, 1882, **John Henry Henshall**
Here, the artist paints women and children in a working-class pub, a sight deplored by those who campaigned against alcohol. Pubs were a centre of community life in Victorian London.

capital. London remained the hub of a global empire, receiving a constant flow of goods and people from around the world. But two world wars left Londoners with a terrible reminder that their city's fortunes could fall as well as rise. 'Blitzkrieg' bombing in the winter of 1940–41 left thousands dead and buildings in ruins.

WEALTHY	
WELL-TO-DO	
COMFORTABLE	
POOR & COMFORTABLE (MIXED)	
POOR	
VERY POOR	
SEMI-CRIMINAL	

Sections from the Map of Poverty, 1886–1903
Charles Booth's survey into life and labour in London mapped the social character of every street in the city. The colour coding represents degrees of poverty and wealth.

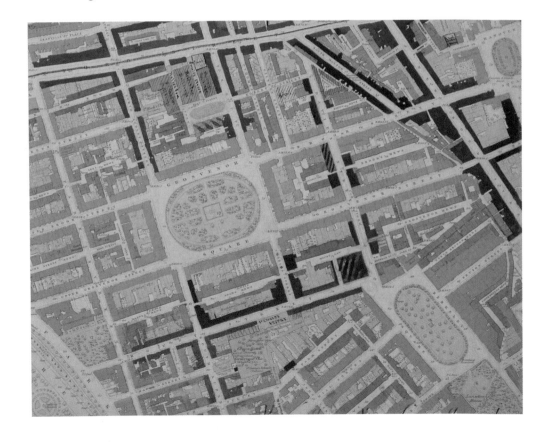

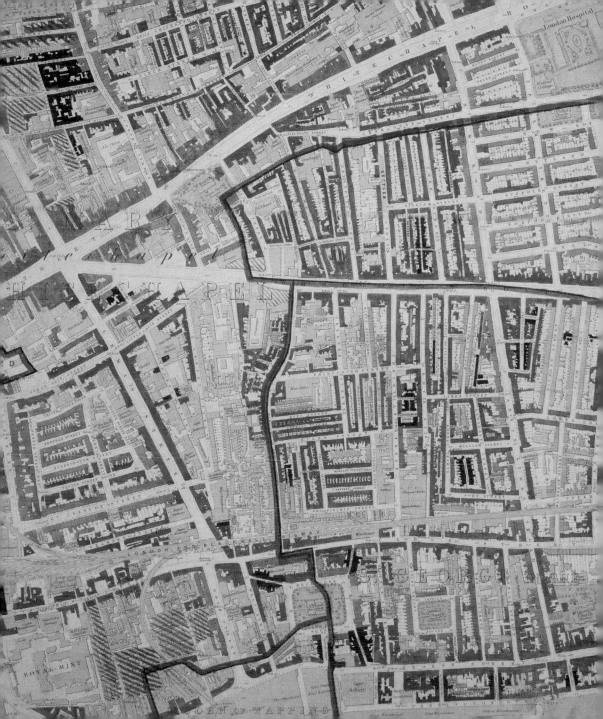

Gold shoes, c.1925
These shoes were made by Ignazio Pluchino. Ignazio was born in Sicily and moved to London in 1900, where he established his business in Chelsea making beautiful shoes for wealthy clients.

Wedding dress made from Indian sari silk, 1931
The fabric was presented to the wife of the headmaster of Highgate School by the Thakur Sahib of Rajkot, to thank her for caring for his son, who died from tuberculosis whilst at the school. In 1931 the fabric was made up into a wedding dress for her daughter.

Marshall & Snelgrove lift panel, 1930s
This Chinese-style panel was part of a lift interior in Marshall & Snelgrove's Oxford Street department store.

Model Y Ford 8 car, 1936
The Model Y Ford 8 was a London made car, one of the first to roll off the assembly line at Ford's newly built Dagenham factory in 1932. It went from drawing board to production in just 10 months.

Selfridges lift, 1928
The American Gordon Selfridge opened his Oxford Street store in 1909. By the 1920s Selfridges was the most glamorous department store in London. Its gilded bronze lift was installed in 1928.

**Women in a Shelter, 1941,
Henry Moore**
Londoners in underground
air-raid shelters, as seen by
the artist Henry Moore. He
described the shelters as a
'huge city in the bowels of
the earth...I was fascinated.
I went back again and again'.

Budge Row, 1944
A rescue party at work after
a V-1 flying bomb exploded.
The man pulled out of the
rubble was one of several
rescued alive.

**War damage in the City
of London, 1940–44**
These photographs were
all taken by two police
constables, Arthur Cross
and Fred Tibbs, who
recorded the damage as it
happened. The view on the
right was taken in January
1941. The bomb had
penetrated the booking
hall of Bank Underground
station, killing 50 people.

**A bombed bus,
9 September 1940**
This bus had been hit by
a high-explosive bomb
falling in the early hours
of the morning.

**Queen Victoria Street,
11 May 1941**
The Salvation Army
Headquarters at
Queen Victoria Street,
photographed just as the
building facade fell.

**St Paul's Cathedral,
10 October 1940**
Showing bomb damage
to the cathedral's roof.

WORLD CITY 1950s–TODAY

During the 1950s London was still recovering after its wartime ordeal. The population had shrunk and there was much to do in the way of reconstruction.

The new London that took shape in the 1950s and 1960s felt very different from its pre-war predecessor. London's old economy faltered as old firms shut up shop and the docks began to close. A youth revolution brought a new energy to London, along with a new obsession with fashion.

Above all, the faces of Londoners changed as people began to move around the world more easily, settling in a city that already had a global dimension. By the end of the twentieth century, London was a truly cosmopolitan world city, diversity at its heart.

As with all world cities, London cannot help but speculate about its future. Climate change poses challenges. How can the city reduce its carbon footprint? Where will the jobs of the future come from? Should London build higher skyscrapers or deeper tube lines? Whatever the future, this inspirational world city will never stand still.

Bill and Ben the Flower Pot Men, 1950s
Bill and Ben were two of the puppet stars of *Watch with Mother*, a children's television programme first screened in the 1950s.

Beatles mini dress, 1964
Worn by Pauline Richey when selling programmes at the premiere of the Beatles' film *Hard Day's Night* at the London Pavilion in 1964.

Mary Quant dress, 1966
Mary Quant opened her
boutique, Bazaar, in the King's
Road in Chelsea in 1955. This
dress is made of bonded
jersey, a fabric very popular in
the 1960s because it did not
crease and held its shape.

Pashmina shawl, 2008
Designed by Alexander
McQueen, the son of a
London taxi driver who
became a global
fashion name. This
print appeared on
many items in his
Autumn/Winter 2008
collection.

'Mayor's chain', 2007
Produced by Tatty
Devine, the trading
name of two former
artists who opened a
shop in East London's
Brick Lane in 2001. The
chain is a quirky version
of a traditional mayoral
chain of office.

***The Sphere*
magazine, 1951**
The cover story
celebrates the
Festival of Britain
exhibition on
London's south
bank. The futuristic
structures and
buildings included
the Dome of
Discovery and the
slender Skylon.

History Painting, 1993–94, John Bartlett

The 'Poll Tax Riot' broke out in Trafalgar Square on Saturday 31 March 1990, as a protest against the new tax. The artist wanted to capture an occasion that had historic significance for London.

Spirit of the Carnival, 1988, Tam Joseph

This print captures the hostility between the police and London's Caribbean community which blighted the Notting Hill Carnival during the 1970s.

Photographs by Henry Grant (1907–2004)
Henry Grant was a photojournalist who worked in London from the 1950s to the 1980s. His entire archive of thousands of images is now held by the Museum.

Badges
A few of the 2,000 badges in the Museum's collections. These examples date from the 1960s to the 1990s. The black and gold badge is 1970s and comes from Biba, the famous London fashion shop.

**London Fields –
The Ghetto, 1994
(part)**
Part of a large
model of Ellingfort
Road and London
Lane in Hackney,
by model-maker
James Mackinnon
and photographer
Tom Hunter. The
two streets were
lived in by
squatters and
were under threat
of demolition at
the time.

**Portraits of the
residents, 1994**
These photographs by Tom
Hunter were intended to
show that the residents of
Ellingfort Road, although
squatters, had spent time and
effort on their homes. Many
had been living there for over
10 years.

Future London, 2008
A view of London's future created by the firm GMJ, from an aerial photograph by Jason Hawkes. It shows the possible effects of extreme climate change and new technologies on the capital.

THE LORD MAYOR'S COACH

'The City' is the capital's historic core, a place steeped in tradition yet ultra-modern. Today, it is famous for international finance, yet many other things happen within its square mile. People live and study there, and thousands of commuters arrive on weekdays to work in shops, sandwich bars and offices.

The Museum's most spectacular exhibit is part of the City's living tradition. The Lord Mayor's State Coach is a superb example of eighteenth-century coach building, and it is still in working order. It leaves the Museum every November to carry the newly elected Lord Mayor through the City streets in the annual Lord Mayor's Show.

The office of Lord Mayor dates back to the twelfth century. The holder is the head of the City of London Corporation and represents the City on national occasions. Since 2000, London has also had a city-wide mayor: this Mayor of London is head of the Greater London Authority, the strategic body for the whole of London.

The Lord Mayor's State Coach
The coach was commissioned in April 1757 from Joseph Berry of Leather Lane, Holborn, for the fixed price of £860. It was finished in record time and was first used in November that year.

THE SACKLER HALL

The Sackler Hall is a space for rest and refreshment on the lower floor of the Museum. At the north end of the Hall, a bank of computer pods enable visitors to find out more about any object on display and browse through our collections' online database. At the south end there is a space for small changing exhibitions on the overall theme of creativity and inspiration. Exhibitions will often include paintings and artworks from the Museum's own collections.

The Bayswater Omnibus, **1895, George William Joy**
A painting inspired by a new form of public transport, a horse-drawn omnibus. The woman with a baby is a portrait of the artist's wife.

MUSEUM OF LONDON DOCKLANDS

If you have enjoyed your journey through London's turbulent past, then why not complete your introduction to the city with a visit to our sister venue, Museum of London Docklands? From Roman settlement to Docklands' regeneration, this 200-year-old warehouse reveals the long history of the capital as a port.

Discover a wealth of objects from whale bones to Second World War gas masks in state-of-the-art galleries, including Mudlarks, an interactive area for children; Sailortown, an atmospheric recreation of nineteenth-century riverside Wapping; and London, Sugar & Slavery, which reveals the city's involvement in the transatlantic slave trade. With ancient finds, unusual objects, fascinating tours and free family events, Museum of London Docklands is one of the capital's hidden treasures.

Open daily 10am – 6pm
(closed 24–26 December)

To find out more call 020 7001 9844 or visit
www.museumoflondon.org.uk/docklands

Museum of London Docklands
West India Quay
London E14 4AL

 West India Quay

 Canary Wharf

 Canary Wharf Pier